On Raven's Wings

On Raven's Wings

Concetta Tina Scarpitti

authorHOUSE®

AuthorHouse™ LLC
1663 Liberty Drive
Bloomington, IN 47403
www.authorhouse.com
Phone: 1-800-839-8640

Published by AuthorHouse   03/17/2014

ISBN: 978-1-4918-1598-4 (sc)
ISBN: 978-1-4918-1597-7 (e)

Library of Congress Control Number: 2013916379

CONTENTS

A Masked Face

Mysterious eyes of disguise
Teardrops fill with secretive cries,
Deep penetrating, solemn thoughts
Mixed emotions, the truth is sought.
Mysterious eyes of disguise
Fading away day by day,
Fears riding the open road delayed
Too late for saving what is truly sane.
Mysterious eyes of disguise
Wandering the night until sunrise,
Unveiling the mask of what was her face
She is now heard by her howling cries.
Mysterious eyes of disguise, a slayer
Her face appears, peeling away every layer,
Harming only the sinful
Evil disappears, wiping away the ungrateful.

Concetta Tina Scarpitti

All of Your Strength

She strives to regain her strength
To move forward, she lacks breath,
Unable to generate another word
She is unaware what has occurred.
Losing the movement in her body so fragile
She is now in tremendous denial,
She is slowly losing her mobility
And becoming more desperate by agility.
Surpassing all that she lived for
She no longer has an open door,
Strength collapses by her fears
And she is convinced she doesn`t have a year.
She strives to regain her strength
To move forward she lacks breath,
Unable to generate another word
She is unaware what has occurred.

Concetta Tina Scarpitti

An Angel with a Beating Heart

Flutter your wings, my angel of wisdom
Spread the glorious love to your people in the kingdom,
Open your heart that's mesmerized by pure gold
Allow the pain to be released and unfold.
Shower your speckled treasures from above
And splash my face with your unconditional love,
Make those who don't know you believe in the miracle
Allow them to see only your silhouette, a true spectacle.
Your love overpowers all hearts in harmony
You were always a blessing, even through a tragedy,
You are my angel who keeps her heart beating
He took away my fears and left me empowering.

Concetta Tina Scarpitti

Blindness

Twitching in your burning eyes, stinging from behind the retina
So painful, you fall to your knees with no stamina,
Trying to allow yourself to stand tall
Pitter, patter, your eyes aglow, remain listening to the endless rainfall.
Every drop, erasing the next one ever so lightly
Dragging your heels in knee-deep,
Teeth gritting lips bleed so slightly
You begin to drown in your eyes as you sleep.
You are standing in an eclipse with a dark shadow of glory
When should you be telling your story?
The truth which lies through the ripple of the waves
What you cannot reverse will remain unscathed.

Concetta Tina Scarpitti

Broken Wings

He curls his long-fingered toes around his needle tree
He caws over his prey and proceeds,
Snatching a ripple of flesh, he dives
This is his only chance to survive.
Unbeckoning calls, he continues his hunt, he stalls
Unwittingly trembling, shivering overall,
It is a chilly night, but very calm indeed
Swinging over his dark shadow of greed.
A prayer is interrupted by the coyotes ahead
Survival is to blame for what's been said,
A neverending success story unless you revive
A lasting moment of being dead or alive.

Concetta Tina Scarpitti

Change

When all around is adapting to change
It's time for us to breakaway from disturbing chains,
When all else fails, you start again
It's time to save the train from its' derail.
Capture the essence of time standing still
Behind the clouds, lies the window opportunity of will,
In your tender grasp, the future lies ahead
You can't take your words back from what was once said.
Don't take for granted any gifts you receive
Instead, take what you can get and you shall believe,
In your inner soul, as you trust only thee
And remember to sow what you keep.
Take the beauty into the palm of your hand
Do not sink into ambiguous quick sand,
Live life to the fullest, and turn every page
And you will survive this inevitable world of change.

Concetta Tina Scarpitti

Crystal Waters

Clear, purity of your enveloping soul
Warm embrace, awash consoled,
Established in its` almighty land
Along the seashore lies the endless sand.
Crystallized patterns lap the miles of shore
Overlapped by the angelic waters` downpour,
Tears fade behind the distinct waves of water
As the sunrays breathe internally, they get warmer.
Sifting the sands of the shore
Opening the heart of the oceans` door,
The crystal waters appear
Refreshing start is veneered.

Concetta Tina Scarpitti

Earth Never Saw the Light

When the trees shrink down to their roots
When the flowers separate from their groups,
When the sea departs from the deepest waters
When the burning sun is no longer hotter.
When the clouds step down from the endless sky
When the message is misread and inevitably lie,
When the earth becomes the moonlight
When the stars stop sparkling from so very high.
When the rainstorm rises up, not down
When the world is said to be flat, not round,
When the soul never leaves your body in every way
When the earth never sees the light, until the very next day.

Concetta Tina Scarpitti

Face To Face

The spoken word has been foretold
You now carry the purity in the centre of a hearts` gold,
The core is what remains with you to hold
As you disappear, a chill of a mighty cold.
As I shiver in mere silence from my Love
The soft music is still playing up above,
Your memory stands still in a time of renaissance
As you take me up to the highest distance.
We feed the birds of an ivory white
We guide each other, a flock blinded by night,
Holding my golden heart, we release our doves
Never letting go until we arrive to the path of Love.
Together we form one direction
Your guidance illuminates our section,
As I stand in your place
We see each other for the second time face to face.

Concetta Tina Scarpitti

Faith

When all else seems surreal
It may be difficult to completely heal,
I pray strongly before the altar of faith
Hands clamping together, I layeth.
We think why these things can be
We ask ourselves the questions before we believe,
Unknowingly doubting the Higher faith
As we absorb ourselves with leftover strength.
We try so much harder to be a purer man
But it doesn't defeat the grasp of His hand,
We can only take the pain to withstand
Every window we open, as He takes an upper hand.

Concetta Tina Scarpitti

Fallen Tree . . .

As I gaze up to the sparkling stars above your tree
I hear your careless whisper to me,
As you reach out to hold my mighty hand
I see your footprints sinking in the endless sand.
As I gaze up to the trickling stars above your tree
I feel your mellow, but beating heartbeat,
As you gaze into my hopeless, glazed eyes,
I am so blinded by the powerful light.
As I gaze up to the illuminating stars above your tree
I pray for only thee,
As I close my restless eyes
I kneel before the burning sunrise.
As I gaze up to the neverending stars above your tree
I awake from my nightmare, which is now a reality,
I blow you a kiss goodnight and weep
As I watch over you, as you fall asleep.

Concetta Tina Scarpitti

Father and Daughter

It is I that aches for you to get well
It is I that wipes away your endless tears,
It is I that held your hand when it swelled
It is I that protected you from your greatest fears.
It is I that let you borrow my shoulder to cry on
It is I that created the road for you to walk along,
It is I that carried you when He snatched you so soon
It is I that showed you the burning sunrise until noon.
It is I that kneels before your grave
It is I that sifts the sand of footsteps wave after wave,
It is now that He stands
He will take you to the forever Promised Land.

Concetta Tina Scarpitti

Garnet Petals

A blooming, garnet-stone petal curls
Renewing its` past with a fresh new day,
I await for every corner to unfurl
Until it has blown completely away.
I blow every crisp petal of garnet red
I squish its` juices and get it all fingerprinted,
It seems to bleed out, dead
I make room for regrowth and dig at its`foot imprint.
Crackling sequence of red fire
I await the dew to waiver its` past growth,
Raindrops put out the fire with no desire
And eats away at its` youth.

Concetta Tina Scarpitti

Heart of Darkness

Deep thoughts folded ever so neatly
Friendly company of deceit,
Ambiguous emotions of love and hate
Uncertain times that lead the present to late.
The heart beats faster without a doubt
Alone and below, the noises get louder and louder,
Return of the favour, hour upon hour
She awaits the temptation of her devour.
The heart of stone has its' chamber open
Darkness unveils nature's scorn,
The throne has a skull and bone
The heart of darkness has been reborn.

Concetta Tina Scarpitti

I Am . . .

Lord, help me to think positively
Lord, tell me I'm beautiful emotionally,
Lord, help me be purely good
Lord, help me be understood.
Lord, I am who I am today
Lord, you are my powerful sunray,
Lord, I am who you've made me to be
Lord, you are my source of energy.
Lord, take away all of my fears
Lord, remove my sins until I see clearly,
Lord, take away all the painful layers beneath
Lord, remove the negativity.
Lord, carry my strength to higher ground
Lord, pray for all who haven't yet found,
Lord, carry my soul, I do confide
Lord, pray for all, my journey alongside.

Concetta Tina Scarpitti

In Time

One step forward, one step behind
When will we ever be able to find,
What we have been searching for so very long
Maybe we'll find the answers at the end of the song.
I capture all reasonings
I capture all destinies,
We seize to search for the ultimate truth
Lying beneath the surface of today's youth.
Until science gives us the answers to find
We may now be in a bind,
One step forward, one step behind
When will we ever be able to find the time?

Concetta Tina Scarpitti

Last Breath . . .

~~~

You held on a little longer
You promised to stay and be stronger,
You tried and tried but soon let go
You followed the light, and left your soul.
Walking behind a shadow of you
I couldn't see, as your footsteps remain only a clue,
I caught up to you or so I thought
Your scent was a sign, I have sought.
My heart was filled with your aroma
My spirit rejoiced to be with you for a moment,
I started to follow your mighty glow
But the cool breath remained, you've let go.

Concetta Tina Scarpitti

Midnight Hue

The crisp, auburn red sun is burning my face
You give me a new breath in every trace,
Your footsteps remain in the sifty sands
You reach out for my praying hands.
You show me you are in a peaceful place
You mark every footprint with every pace,
You whisper my name with the greatest Love
You then disappear up and above.
Thank-you for letting me see your spiritual face
Thank-you for ensuring me your secure place,
Thank-you for warming my cupped hands
Thank-you for drying my tears from my eyes.

Concetta Tina Scarpitti

Mildew Drops

The rain splashes over my face
Renewing my existing place,
Extracting my footsteps retrace
Refreshing mildew, petals of lace.
The rain pours down its` almighty plea
Encircling, crystal drops fall, one, two, three,
Puddles deepen, their strengths` open their arms so openly
Entangling me in the dew trees` branches so strongly.
Precipitation washes my eyes
My feelings and gestures are in disguise,
Mildness turns to a sun that rises
I breathe in the warm air of dryness.

Concetta Tina Scarpitti

On Raven's Wings

Spread out like the Goddess of Love
Escaping sin, He enters the gallows of graphite stone,
He puts forth His niche, a charcoaled dove
He settles into His prey, a granite throne.
Tilting His crooked neck on an angle
He allows His curiosity to get the better of Him,
He paces before the hidden traps of mangle
He doesn't respond to goodness, only sin.
He is trapped before the Darkness settles in
He agrees to absolve sins if you let Him go,
He knows He's lost, doesn't surrender and doesn't win
He is the only splattered mark on the icy sheet of snow.

Concetta Tina Scarpitti

Only Time Will Tell

As the hand strikes its' face
Time moves forward and takes her place,
As the hand ticks over to the next number
She holds her breath, from Spring to Summer.
As the hand moves forward
She strikes over by one, two, three . . .
As the hand stands by its' sword
It strikes sharply on its' degree.
As the hand rotates on its' axis
The past meets the future of fact,
As the hand steps on its' own max
Pointing away from almost to exact.

Concetta Tina Scarpitti

Rebirth

The splash of freshwater tide
Engulfing the aura off to her side,
Tears run down her joyous face
As she gives birth to the human race.
Ripple of waves erupt the flow
Illuminating her features and expressing her glow,
She appears on the horizon, a burning sight
Transitioning her rotating axis from day to night.
She takes another breath above the burning water
As the sand sifts up above sea level, getting hotter,
Burning sands of glory
Renewing another life of ancient history.

Concetta Tina Scarpitti

Shoreline

Time expires as the years go by
The waters overlap natures` shoreline,
Days turn to restless nights
The sky meets the endless sunrise.
Clear, blue waters of a fallen cascade
Deep oceans, sharp-tide blades,
Overturn the strength of its` tides
The rocks kiss natures` waters so very high.
The sun burns the waters of deep
The shadows of footsteps lie on sands so steep,
The air is crisp, as a blanket of linen
The sheets of sand lie next to the sun made to glisten.
The beach kisses the shoreline
The stars twinkle the sky line of tigers` eye,
The sea has hues of emerald green so very fine
Hear the sand kiss the shoreline in overtime.

Concetta Tina Scarpitti

Silhouette of Your Face

The irridescent rainbow splashes over the mountain ice-glacier scene
The rain feeds its` thirst on the frozen rocks so surreal,
The mountain top kisses the illuminating sun so clearly
The unbearable heat is burning like melted steel.
The acoustic voices erupt in the crisp crust between the earth
The overlapping waves kiss the sea against the rocks I appeal,
The hues combine and form a rainbow of mirth
The tide is moving in, so serene.
The ice caps volcanically erupt and wake up the pillars
The reproduction of natures` place,
The moonlight glowing overpowers the stars
Your silhouette appears, the silhouette of your untouchable face.

Concetta Tina Scarpitti

Soul of the Night

He surpasses the goal
By removing what he stole,
A gallow stands still under the silver moon
All sound is silent, so prevalent.
Disaster can't strike twice or can it?
Souls are resting so peacefully, I sit,
Awaiting my own destiny
It seems I'm waiting an eternity.
The silver lining of the moon outlines her shadow
He grasps all his might to take her to the gallows,
Gripping with all of his might
He has taken it, the soul of the night.

Concetta Tina Scarpitti

Stitched Lips

Your words are sitting alone on the empty throne
It is not a belief I do condone,
I am uncertain of spoken words from generous lips, I trace
As thine arms embrace at a slower pace.
Escaping from a runaway place
Releasing the chains of a broken space,
Surrounded by negative energy of defeat
Pretending the untouched is secure and neat.
Deadly markings still sit on the sands
Spoiled by the activity of dirty, stained hands,
Unexplained tampering, unchartered waters unstitch her lips
Leaving her tears behind, and begin the laughter slip.

Concetta Tina Scarpitti

Thank-you Father

⁓

Your eyelashes fall down one by one
You always knew how to teach the words of wisdom,
You made me happy with every shining smile
And reminded me that I was your favourite little girl.
You allowed me to express myself
You taught me how rich life was without wealth,
You pronounced my first spoken word, `Papa`
You teased mom so proudly which ended in laughter.
You made me what I am today
You are my standing ground, my rock, my clay,
You made me feel special when we danced the night away
And welded me a steel flower arch for my perfect wedding day.
You are forever, my dear Father
A kind hearted knight in shining armour,
``Mio bello papa,`` just a token to say thank-you for your guiding hands
I shall raise the dissipated ashes into crystallized sands.
``Papa, grazie per la cresciuta.``
``Dad, thanks for raising me, as I take care of mom as I promised.``

Concetta Tina Scarpitti

The Lord Hath Spoken

The Lord gives thine `tis hand
The Lord gathers the seeds of His land,
The Lord awaits your undying Fate
The Lord takes `tis brush and begins to paint.
The Lord has opened up a whole new day
The Lord reads the words to say,
``I pour my adoration over and above``
His wings open with porous Love.
The Lord guides thine own soul
The Lord opens `tis arms to console,
The Lord hath spoken the words of wisdom
The Lord hath given us the Life of reason.

Concetta Tina Scarpitti

The Silver Moon

Glistening in the limelight
She motions her movement, out of sight,
She opens her green eyes, a might glow
Gleaming the icy waters of deep below.
Sharp waves of icy calm
Shattered glass evaporates in my palm,
A mighty hand, an unreachable fear
A mighty war resonates, it soon appears.
A battle breaks its' barriers
Relapsing the stars, layer by layer,
Reappearing before my very eyes
A presence of sweet disguise.
Beaming over the neverending pier
The darkness unknown, overlapping with fear,
The touch of a sparkling glimmer of steel
The silver moon stands alone, so surreal.

Concetta Tina Scarpitti

Waiting for a Sign

Sweet, succulent gumdrops surround your oak tree
Underground of six feet deep,
This is the paradise you chose to be
Where the sunshine illuminates its` seeds.
Angels lurk amongst the silky silhouette
Shadows are overpowering your angel sight,
I think of our first meeting when we met
Now the beauty of day turns to a mighty cold night.
I sit patiently for your whisper
Filling the purity in my emptied heart,
Shivering as the petals are, an aged petal gets crispier
Filling my heart with warmth, a spirit appears in the midnight dark.
Darkness prevails under the clouds of wonder
The moon glows in the midst and winks freely,
I sit awaiting your sign as I ponder
Now I know you have reached me.

Concetta Tina Scarpitti

Waters of Deep

Broken glass scatters amongst the stormy waves
Drowning her sorrows in a shallow grave,
Shadows of dark, cut inside like a knife
Emotions tangled in a web, out of sight.
A hidden agenda covers up her true self
An old testament still remains on her shelf,
A partial truth sets her degree
Broken chains, now break her free.
Breathable circumstance of choice
Benefitting the ultimate source,
A dart does not centre itself
With no sweat, nor tears does one ever make wealth.

Concetta Tina Scarpitti

About the Author

Concetta Tina Scarpitti, born and raised in Toronto, Ontario with her five siblings, Joe, Angela, Tom, Mitz and Tony, along with her niece, Ashley Samantha Lo Russo, the distinguished Artist. Concetta enjoys oil painting, collecting old war coins, and practicing karate kata forms. Concetta would like to thank her travelling sisterhood of librarian friends, you know who you are, who have supported her throughout this process, my sister-in-law, Angie, "my rockstar," and Authorhouse's Design Team and distinguished consultants. And I'd like to thank my husband, Steve for supporting me throughout this process. "Happy 15th Anniversary, and I'll always be your lady of your heart."

Much thanks!